Finance 7 Tricks for International Property Investors

VOLUME 1

First published in 2022

Sherwood Finance Limited
4/129 Kensington High Street
London W8 6BD England

The moral rights of the authors have been asserted.

ISBN: 978-0-6454035-8-9 (pbk)

Contents

Introduction

Financing properties can be daunting to inexperienced eyes, especially as changes to financing criteria and regulations have been introduced since the pandemic. For this reason, lenders must know the varying requirements in different countries. We face many obstacles including languages, time zones, and lending markets. We can get the most from the market in any location with contacts worldwide. Our Mortgage Guide for international investors covers the wide variety of mortgage terms and finances available, as well as information on where you can get the world's most outstanding property locations. We will investigate fantastic options in areas like.

Algarve & Quint do Lago, the French Alps, Sydney, Côte d›Azur, Dubai, St Barts, Marrakech, Rome and Milan, Melbourne, New York, Geneva, Lake Como, Lisbon, the Bahamas, Amsterdam, London, Marbella and Balearics, Zürich, Monaco, and Lugano. Those locations are attractive, but far from all.

Different mortgage options

Working with clients' advisors and private banks

We tailor the mortgage arrangements we make to our client's needs, and because of this, we often work with private banks. We do everything in our power to make sure that we can get the ideal mortgage for our clients — and one way that we do this is by working with the client's tax advisors. Sherwood Finance is experienced in home loans of all shapes and sizes, from complex and bespoke mortgages to traditional ones. We also understand how crucial it can be to pick the right mortgage for their needs, regardless of their financial situation, plans, and more. We may have limited direct contact with clients depending on their relationship with their advisors, but we will offer the same quality service, regardless.

High-value home loan

In the United Kingdom, home loans of £1 million+ are now more common than ever. Various loan suit individuals seeking increased financing, such as private bank mortgages, equity release, high-value mortgages, and home loans secured by assets. We tailored most of these mortgages to suit the investor's needs, often considering their earnings, support, and more. Our team of specialists works with over three hundred lenders, ensuring that we can get the best possible terms for our clients.

Bridging loan

From refurbishment to development funding, several loans come under the umbrella of bridging finance. In most cases, these loans have short terms, and while this can be quite a challenge for borrowers, it can certainly be possible to achieve excellent terms with flexibility. In addition, many crucial things to bridging finance deals, such as competitive interest rates, using assets and income as security, and staged funding (to save on interest). Our experts are more than capable of helping clients with all of this and other areas of bridging financing, like pre-arranging a cheaper refinancing at the end of the loan's term.

International mortgage financing

The mortgage market in the UK is liquid — which is quite the opposite of several European countries. It's one of the main reasons we work with international and

UK contacts; to help our clients secure a mortgage in any country. We understand and appreciate the unique property regulations in different areas, often resulting in a more secure loan. We work across the globe too, over the years, we have given countless individuals of varying nationalities the chance to secure a home loan.

Mainstream home loans

Mainstream mortgages are still an excellent choice for many clients — and while we often work with private banks, we can also secure traditional home loans. Mainstream financing can sometimes be complex (especially with a high-value loan), but most of them only need standard mortgage funding and can be taken care of by a traditional bank. With our experience and knowledge, our team is more than capable of securing the best possible terms.

Things that could affect your application

Several factors can affect a funding application, which can be categorised into four separate groups:

Your finances

All mortgages need the borrower to pay off their debt and cover the set payments of the loan. This relies on a regular income, but our goal is to fund individuals with irregular or limited income with significant security assets. You will find that we can help anyone, so whether you want a traditional mortgage or a unique arrangement to suit your needs, we are here to help.

Compliance requirements

Our advice can be invaluable for whether a client has a more complicated situation or minor compliance issues. For example, most lenders often need different protocols for a transaction and, as a result, have varying documentation requirements. In most instances, you will find that you need passports, proof of residency/ address, and more. Luckily for you, we have a great deal of experience and knowledge in compliance — which can often be critical to the result. With an understanding of what different lenders need, we put together clients and the ideal parties for their unique circumstances.

The criteria of our clients and lenders

Finding the right investor can be crucial, whether you need a standard or bespoke mortgage loan. To help unite clients with their ideal lenders, we take the time to get all the information we need (from their requirements to their financial landscape). We also consider the prerequisites of varying lenders, ranging from LTVs (Loan to Value) to security assets. So, we know what types of borrowers each investor or lender is looking for and what they offer our clients. This is how we begin negotiations for practical terms for everyone.

Security assets

A traditional mortgage will use the purchased building as security for the loan but is not always ideal sometimes. The property's value, location, and condition are crucial factors to consider. In addition, most lenders hire the services of a surveyor to evaluate the building to check there is anything that could harm the monetary value of the equity. As a result, there may be times where an investor will need more assets to be used as a guarantee, but we will be on your side to help you pick the best solution.

London, United Kingdom

The multicultural characteristics of London are just one of the many things that make this location so prevalent among buyers. People agree this city is the leading financial centre of the globe. With the entire United Kingdom, most would describe London as a property market within a property market. The UK follows the city's lead, observing real estate prices.

Brexit has caused a few challenges over the years — with many residential home buyers retreating. In addition, tax changes have affected the upper end of the real estate market. But the good news things are looking brighter, with UK base rates being just above historic lows and a variety of incredible mortgage deals available.

The British Pound (or sterling) has fallen by circa 20% compared to leading international currencies because of the EU (European Union) referendum in 2016. This has allowed buyers worldwide to get superb residential its properties for less when converting into their currency. Along with deflation in the city's property prices over the years, has increased the percentages of overseas investments for high–end properties–and it is likely to continue.

Individuals have tried to discount the ultra-prime property market in London. But it still attracts plenty of attention, both in the UK and overseas. Our team communicates with several banks and niche lenders, all of which are more than happy to accept clients from across the globe. In addition, the historically low rates have encouraged more people to buy, which has led most lenders to be more competitive. So, you will find London has fantastic mortgage rates to offer — and this, alongside the long-term value of the luxury residential property market here, is perfect for a variety of people.

Things to keep in mind:

▸ Private banks in London lend an LVR of 60-65%, although they can offer as high as 85%. An AUM may not always be necessary, but you should know that it could cost 30% of the loan amount or even a flat price of £500,000 if required. This is when clients want to improve their interest rate or have a more complex profile.

▸ You are likely to find that buy-to-let mortgage loans have an LVR of 65-75% and that loans are often based on the property's rental income. Because of this, the rental potential should cover 100-150% of the mortgage repayments, although this may not be as important for many clients.

▸ You may find lenders have specific criteria depending on varied factors, like your age or nationality. Enough income or wealth often allow individuals to avoid this.

Paris, France

Paris is most famous for being one of Europe's major cities and the home of incredible art, fine dining, and fashion. This location has long been one of the most prominent tourist destinations, and because of this, domestic and international property investments here are standard. Foreign investors were not welcomed in the past, but attitudes have changed in recent years. The election of President Macron was the beginning of a whole new culture, where residents had a more friendly approach to overseas investors.

Since Brexit, France's position in the EU has been significantly boosted, and it is now considered the financial centre of Europe. This has attracted the attention of more investors than ever before — making the country (especially Paris) more attractive to those with an impressive net worth. This, alongside the liquid property market in this city and historically low base rates from the European Central Bank, has only increased domestic and international purchases of select residential properties.

In the global league table of the world's wealthiest investors, Paris has overtaken London. The combination of the country's significant presence in the EU, a more robust economy, and the tax breaks from the current president have made this location so attractive. As a result, the United Kingdom's government has encouraged investors to leave France for the UK, but the situation has changed because of the events of recent years.

Those looking for properties have always been likely to find a variety of options in Paris, but it has only become more popular as socialist influences have lessened. Paris is the most liquid property market in France. Those looking for more competitive terms and lower processing times could learn more about the subtle differences.

Things to keep in mind:

▸ We know the property market in Paris for being more liquid than any other of France's hotspots. Because of this, the mortgage service is more efficient.

▸ Many prime locations that offer sun or ski facilities are seasonal, since rentals in Paris are popular all year round, which means more profit.

▸ Certain parts of the buying process, instructing a notary, may confuse for international customers, which is why proper advice is always recommended.

▸ Typically, legal fees and taxes here are between 3.5 and 7.5 per cent.

Côte d'Azur, France

For many years now, the Côte d'Azur (also known as the French Riviera) has attracted attention of investors. In south-eastern France on the Mediterranean coast, this area is home to Cannes, St Tropez, Monaco, and many more luxury resorts. With France's influence and international stature in the EU, ultra-prime residential property markets across the country have certainly seen a boost, with the French Riviera included.

For most individuals, there are various excellent property investment opportunities in Côte d'Azur. Of course, the prices in the major resorts of the region are high. Still, several more affordable holiday properties are located away from the hustle and bustle of central locations. But we may see an increase in long-term property prices soon, with the demand in these locations growing significantly. The Côte d'Azur is undoubtedly an attractive location for several reasons: the Mediterranean lifestyle and beauty of the many impressive sites, like the F1 Monaco Grand Prix.

The reason property investments in this region are so favoured is the recent changes to the French tax system — although the French Riviera has been attractive to investors for much longer. The changes to the taxation system in France have also influenced how welcoming the French mortgage market is towards international investors. With such high demand in the region, a liquid property market is more crucial.

You will find the most incredible properties available in Côte d'Azur are in areas like Cannes, Monaco, and St Tropez. But, outside of these major resorts, you will find a range of excellent investment opportunities just waiting to be taken. Considering everything this region offers, from luxury living to the climate, is it any wonder why so many investors choose properties here?

Things to keep in mind:

- ▸ You will find that the property market is more liquid than in several other areas in the country, as the French Alps. This means there are chances for individuals to invest in properties without needing AUM — which is ideal for anyone who is not too keen on having a private banking relationship.

- ▸ For those prepared to strike up a new deal, benefits like the chance to secure a loan with a 100% gross LVR basis and the lender needing an investment of just 20% of the mortgage amount for the duration of their client's home loan. This percentage could be even less for individuals with a more diverse range of assets.

▸ As with Paris, the legal fees and taxes can be between 3.5-7.5%.

*Project fees can include notary fees, rolled-up interest, acquisition fees, and more.

French Alps

In the French Alps, you will find that the demand for ski chalets is consistent. Because of this, most find that investments in these types of assets are profitable and secure, too. In addition, many beauties of the region are the unique lifestyle, stunning environment, and peace and relaxation. For these reasons and more, the properties are often highly desirable — even if a short supply of them are on the market. Because of this, most will find that purchasing a property here is not always the easiest of tasks.

You will see several similarities between the different luxury property markets around the globe. Many people choose locations for features like climate, lifestyle, privacy, and secure property values — all of which are good on their own but even better together. In addition, the French Alps border the Italian and Swiss Alps, making the location even more appealing.

With French financial institutions now more accommodating (as mentioned above), international investors are better received. Still, crucial for those hoping to buy to be sensitive to local ideals and procedures when securing a home loan. For example, there is a high demand for luxury ski chalets, which is why investors will need to act fast if they want to buy a property when it becomes available. Even a slight delay in securing the loan could distinguish between buying and missing a fantastic opportunity. On the bright side, the more liquid market is ideal among domestic French banks, international banks, and lenders.

Too many, we consider this region the peak of the country's ultra-prime property market. Few parts of the world offer as much variation in luxury properties as France. There is something for everyone, with locations like Paris, Côte d'Azur, and the French Alps offering a unique way of life. As a result, domestic and international investors are showing more interest in buying a home here than ever.

Things to keep in mind:

▶ Mid-sized mortgages for chalets in hotspots like Morzine and Chamonix are more popular among retail banks. Lenders here will offer higher LVR and credit-only relationships, often negating the need for an AUM.

▶ Those who opt to work with a private bank may not have a choice but to place an AUM since they often only lend here to manage their client's assets.

- Most investors will find that seasonal letting will be profitable.

- The legal fees and taxes are somewhere between 3.5 and 7.5% *Project fees can include notary fees, rolled-up interest, acquisitions, and more.

Monaco, French Riviera

In the Côte d'Azur, Monaco is famous for its property market and investors. With real estate prices being so high (with costs per square foot being the highest globally), it is not surprising to see the premier location for people with a high net worth. It is well known for Monte Carlo having a variety of luxury boutiques, hotels, restaurants, and much more. In addition, the F1 Grand Prix is held in the city's streets, and the event is broadcast worldwide. Monaco is famous for its attractions and investment opportunities.

At the French Mediterranean coastline, it is easy to believe that Monaco is home to more millionaires than any other city in the world. As a result, this city-state has a reputation unlike any other in the property market. The supply of properties is low, but the demand is high. Sometimes, the property costs are so high that even wealthy investors may need to secure more finance when purchasing here.

The good news is that most lenders offer competitive mortgage loan rates because these states hold their value and have an exorbitant amount of stability. Because of this, while waiting for properties to become available, many individuals use this time wisely and arrange finance terms ready for when the time comes. Even the slightest delay could make you miss an incredible opportunity, which is why it can be so important to be prepared to invest.

The beautiful climate, ideal lifestyle, incredible tax situation, and more are just a few of the things that make Monaco so appealing to investors across the globe. It is also the ideal location for those who want confidential property ownership. But consider strict requirements for living in Monaco.

Things to keep in mind:

▸ With incredible stability and value in real estate, an extensive range of competitive lenders in multiple jurisdictions.

▸ When applying for residency in Monaco, it is necessary to deposit at least €500,000 in a bank. A private bank can take this as collateral, which can be accepted for the property loan.

▸ Like Paris, Monaco's limited supply of real estate causes suspensive clause conditions to be put in place. This delays sales and protects buyers if they are refused a mortgage and cannot buy a property in cash. Often, getting ahead and starting your mortgage application can help to prevent any issues later.

▸ Overall, Monaco's legal fees and taxes are circa 6%

▸ *Project fees can include notary fees, rolled-up interest, acquisitions, and more.

Marbella and Balearic, Spain

Marbella and the Balearic Islands (home to Ibiza, Menorca, and Mallorca, to name a few) have long been desirable by property investors. The last ten years have not been ideal, though, primarily because of the recession caused by the pandemic. But it is important to note that the property market in Spain has seen difficulties — more so than most other parts of the globe.

There may be signs that the Spanish property market will eventually recover, but the sales and prices in the regions of the Balearics and Marbella have been strong through these times. As a result, most will be pleased to hear that real estate prices and transaction numbers have increased immensely recently.

Since the economic downturn, the Spanish government has encouraged overseas property investments. This has enabled the prices in Marbella and the Balearic Islands to increase. This does not mean there are not any good deals waiting in these regions; in fact, most will find excellent value here, especially at the higher end of the spectrum. The houses in this part of Spain are desirable with the peaceful lifestyle, stunning climate, and friendly locals.

Individuals have been more aware of the broader Spanish property market. Many Spanish banks have many unwanted buildings in their books that they have been putting on the market hoping to make sales. But most will find that it's not the case in the Balearics and Marbella. The last decade was difficult for the country, but there are signs of improvement with more transactions, more expensive properties, and more available home loans. Many professionals believe Spain is undervalued and has excellent long-term value — which could be taken advantage of.

Things to keep in mind:

▸ An increasing number of retail banks here are offering investors dry loans.

▸ In prime areas like Marbella and the Balearic Islands, interest-only mortgages from international private banks are more available, especially for liquid and diversified individuals.

▸ Many private international banks also offer 100% gross LVR home loans, although this needs 40% AUM. A good option for those who want to ease Inheritance Tax liability.

▸ The legal fees and taxes are often between 7.5% and 10%.

Geneva, Switzerland

At the southern end of Lake Geneva, the city of Geneva is one of Switzerland's most prominent locations. Low tax rates, high living standards, and a stable economy are just a few things that draw investors' attention. In addition, the scenery, and views here are magnificent, as the Alps and the Jura mountains surround the city. As a result, there has been high demand in Geneva for years now, with property prices steadily increasing over the last two decades.

You will notice the city's heavy French influence, from the gastronomy to the language. The headquarters of the European United Nations and the Red Cross are located here, which is one reason this city is a hub for global diplomacy. There is plenty to love, from the incredible sights to the culture. All this has attracted the attention of countless investors. Geneva has such a high density of millionaires that Monaco is the only location to have more.

The financial sector in this city is robust, as you can imagine. The best part of this is that it also ensures a good supply of opportunities for individuals to get mortgage loans for luxury homes. The demand for real estate here has been high for many years, partially because of Switzerland's property market regulation. Each administrative region here has their own rules and regulations. For this reason alone, it can often be a wise idea to hire the help of a mortgage broker with experience in the mortgage procedures of specific areas.

In recent years, the demand for properties has decreased, attributed to the location drawing the awareness of many individuals looking to invest. Geneva is home to a variety of incredible jewellers, fine dining establishments, excellent hotels. While the mortgage market is heavily regulated, it is important to note that there are still many excellent luxury properties available here that you could profit from.

Things to keep in mind:

▸ Investors need to consider a cap on the number of properties foreign buyers can buy each year. The way to work around this is to have a Swiss residency permit.

▸ Despite heavy regulations, the low-interest rates and remarkable properties in this destination make it worthwhile for most investors.

▸ It is essential to consider the internal administrative structure of the country, as there are 26 "cantons", each of which has its own set of rules and regulations. For example, notary fees can work out to be more expensive.

▸ You are likely to find that the legal fees and taxes are between 3.5% and 5%

Zürich, Switzerland

With quality of life, Zürich is often considered one of the world's best cities. Lake Geneva, Zürich, is known for luring investors who want to live here and those who want to invest in property. The history, culture, and lifestyle are significant characteristics of the city, but one of the biggest draws is a global centre for banking and finance.

As with the rest of Switzerland, the mortgage market is highly regulated, and most foreign buyers will need to have local authorisation to buy real estate here. Since the rules and regulations vary from one region to the next, it is crucial to understand the procedures to avoid difficulties later. In addition, for buying luxury properties, the home loans here are often incredibly liquid, and Switzerland is considered the home of private banking. Because of this, investors must try to negotiate for the best deals — and with mortgage funding rates being at historic lows, you will be able to get a great short, medium, or long-term rate.

Many will agree that there is plenty to love about Zürich, from the perfect climate and relaxed lifestyle to the entrepreneurism. While climate change in the world may be an issue, those living here will enjoy the beautiful summers and comfortable winters on offer. Most of the population lives in long-term rental accommodation, ideal for investors. The culture in this city is plain to see.

Many investors look to the property sector in the city, although you might find that there are a variety of great opportunities across the region. Not only that, but the low mortgage rates here make investing in Zürich more attractive — although overseas buyers must understand the procedures they need to follow. None can deny that this location has plenty to offer, from the liquid and broad financial sector to the beauty of the region's scenery.

Things to keep in mind:

▸ We can extend the term on a capital repayment home loan for as long as needed, which can generate loan payback of as little as 1% of the original mortgage yearly.

▸ Switzerland has the lowest interest rates on loans in Europe.

▸ Investors have found that the change in the value of the Swiss Franc has had quite an impact on buying. Most have switched to the private sector from retail banks to borrow a stronger currency while avoiding placing an AUM for the loan while converting their domestic currency.

▸ Legal fees and taxes in this city are often between 3.5% and 5%

Lugano, Switzerland

In the south of Switzerland, Lugano is a city that, when compared to Geneva and Zürich, seems small. But, regardless of size, Lugano is one of the country's most popular destinations for several reasons, including beautiful lakeside scenery, traditional cobbled streets, and much more. Switzerland has a clear French influence, but most will find that Lugano has a more Italian atmosphere. This city has Italy's most remarkable features, from the food to the architecture.

Despite its small size, Lugano is an important financial centre for Switzerland. Locations with an incredible prime property market will have an active and liquid financial market. This is because it ensures that home loans are available for investors to buy properties in the region. Well known for the country with a sizeable private banking sector, which only helps those looking to get mortgage deals with security.

Lugano is not as spoken about as cities like Geneva, although this city has much more sun (with an average of 400 more hours of sunshine in total). The positioning of this city puts it at the centre of Europe, so it should come as no surprise that there is an excellent travel network here, which covers the West, Southeast, and North of Switzerland. The city airport is ideal for those who want to travel quickly from the country. Another thing to consider is that Switzerland is the 7th safest place globally — and Lugano has an even lower crime rate than other parts of the country.

The property market here is known for being competitive, with apartments with lakeside views often sell for at least 1 million Swiss Francs. As with other parts of the country, there are regional differences in property ownership and purchases rules and regulations. Because of this, understanding the local procedures and laws is often a necessity. This fantastic location is beautiful, offers an incredible lifestyle, and so much more — so it is easy to see why it attracts so many investors.

Things to keep in mind:

▸ For the most competitive credit offerings, most lenders will need an investment of at least 1 million Swiss Francs to open an account with you.

▸ We can cater to most nationalities, although it is essential to keep in mind that specific lenders only make their loans available to non-Western investors unless they are a tax resident in Switzerland.

▸ You will find that the legal fees and taxes here are often somewhere between 3.5% and 5%

Amsterdam, Netherlands

Amsterdam the capital of the Netherlands is a popular tourist destination, The endless lanes ways covered by cobbled streets and lined by the fascinating architecture that stretches along the canals. It's known for its tolerance, vertical living, diversity and rich culture. But most famous for its Van Gogh and Rembrandt museums, international restaurants and cycling culture, there's little automobile traffic which adds to the tranquillity. Hiring a bicycle or a canal ride is a trendy way to see the city.

Almost everybody admires the remarkable Architecture and it's great for foreign investors because they are welcomed with fewer restrictions. The Netherlands is well known for its major diplomatic hub at the Hague, the international criminal, and justice court, and is the fourth major centre for the United Nations after Geneva, New York, and Vienna.

The real estate panorama of the Netherlands does have its ins and outs. For example, they expect EU citizens to have lived in the Netherlands for at least six months, possess a citizen service number (BSN) and have permanent employment in the country. Besides the above, non-EU citizens might also need to prove that their residence permits can be extended.

Things to keep in mind.

▸ Estimate 6% of the purchase price for fees, including transfer tax (overdrachtsbelasting), legal fees, registration fees and estate agent fees.

▸ There are no restrictions placed on foreigners and non-Dutch residents buying property. But, since the 2008 economic crisis, it has been more difficult to get a Dutch mortgage.

▸ Through our association with a residential property consultancy in Amsterdam, Sherwood Finance offers a varied portfolio of modern apartments to historic canal-side houses. Begin your Netherlands property search now or contact one of our property Finance experts for a more detailed discussion of your requirements.

Sydney, Australia

Most famous for possessing the Harbour Bridge and the Opera house. Sydney has transformed into an upcoming international city. The harbourside city boasts a satisfying beachside vibe and the chance to experience countless beaches within the vicinity of the city. If you want to spend the day walking the old town's cobbled streets on the rocks or on the beach. The city offers thriving entertainment, great sporting events, diverse culture, and consistent sun throughout the summer.

The real estate prices in Sydney have surpassed the likes of New York and Paris. Featuring the most expensive properties around its inner-city harbour. The region has received far more foreign investment than any other state in Australia. As a result, Sydney remains Australia's elite housing market and is considered the financial hub of the continent. In recent years, even regional towns such as Bryon Bay have A list celebrities are competing for its beachside real estate.

To take part in or bid at a residential auction, potential buyers must register by showing identification and will be given a bidder's number. The auctioneer oversees the bidding process. The vendor sets the reserve price before the auction and is entitled to one vendor bid. If they do not reach the reserve price, the highest bidder can negotiate with the sales agent. Unless agreed before the auction, a ten per cent deposit at the fall of the hammer is standard. Make sure finances are ready as they exchanged contracts on the day. Dummy bids are illegal.

Private treaty offers can be verbal or in writing. Although making a formal offer, the vendor is more likely to accept. When the vendor accepts your offer, a five-day cooling-off period begins. They do not bound the buyers and sellers until they exchanged signed contracts. Then titles are prepared. The buyer must pay a deposit. The settlement process can be completed within 30–90 days.

Melbourne, Australia

The city of Melbourne offers not your typical Australian climate or inner-city beaches. Still, it makes up by hosting the world's top sporting events, Grand Prix, Australian Open and the AFL Grand Final, plus weekend getaways to Port Phillip Bay or the Mornington Peninsula, and even the bustling Crown Casino. With these benefits, it's hard not to consider Melbourne for your property investment.

In recent years, Victoria has seen significant population growth, which generated an under-supply of housing. But Victorians have experienced the longest enforced lockdown in the world. So, its residents have been running for the hills and moving across its borders. But the demand for residential real estate in Melbourne will remain strong well into the future.

At the start of the auction, there is no need to register your intent to bid unless it is a condition imposed by the real estate agency. Only the auctioneer may make a vendor bid, and they must announce a 'vendor bid.' If a co-owner intends to bid, the auctioneer must show this at the commencement of the auction. Bidders can ask during the auction if the property is 'on the market.' law prohibits Dummy bids. For mortgagee sales, Deceased estates or Family Law Matters, the property must go to auction; therefore, the agent cannot convey offers before the auction date.

For a private treaty, the Estate Agents Professional Conduct Regulations 2018 state all offers must be communicated unless instructed to the contrary in writing by the vendor. Besides written submissions, buyers can also make verbal offers. If you want the vendor to take you, send a completed contract for sale and offer a deposit. After the vendor accepts your offer, your offer becomes binding only when you and the vendor exchange contracts, and a deposit (10%) is accounted for.

Things to keep in mind

▸ Non-residents must seek FIRB approval before taking an interest in any Australian residential property. Under the FIRB rules, a claim can include but is not limited to signing an unconditional contract agreeing to buy a dwelling or share in a residence.

▸ Due to fast-paced markets may be worth considering a Buyer's Agent.

▸ Government fees are equal to approx. 5 per cent

- Sometimes, weak valuations can lead to limited financing options for overseas investors. Typically, mortgages here are only available from private banks – and they will only lend to liquid investors.

- There's not a wide selection of lenders offering to fund foreign investors

Lake Como, Italy

The natural beauty of the Lombardy region in Northern Italy is fantastic — and while there are many stunning areas in this location, none are as spectacular as Lake Como. The scenery is breath taking, from the unique lake to the foothills of the Alps. The elegant way of living is another reason countless investors are interested in the property market here. There is an array of stunning villas in Lake Como, although you may find that purchasing one is far from a simple task.

The demand for luxury real estate in Lake Como has increased over the years. Investors from around the globe came here looking for a peaceful home after the 2008 US mortgage crisis. These days, properties here are bought from the market not long after they have been put up for sale — with many buyers aiming to buy off-plan structures. The major help of buying one of these estates is that it gives the chance to create the ideal house for their unique requirements.

One of the most attractive things about this region is its natural beauty and serenity. The authorities have put measures in place to limit the number of greenfield sites here to make sure that there is not too much construction in the future, hoping to preserve Lake Como's scenery. Because of this, many foreign investors are keen to renovate and upgrade the properties here. Typically, the procedures and regulations need property owners to have renovation plans cleared by local authorities before they begin.

The mortgage market in Italy is not as liquid as other countries, like the UK, for example, but many find that the increasing property demand in Lake Como is perfect for investing. The costs of purchasing here have been increasing over the last few years. The competition between international lenders is high, too — ideal for ensuring that they get good terms on their mortgage.

Things to keep in mind:

▸ The climate here is ideal for investors looking for a long rental season.

▸ The luxury property market has plenty of potentials, with villas rented out for €100,000+ a week.

▸ You could get a 100% LVR loan on a capital repayment basis — although this will need 40% of the loan amount to be invested with the lender for the mortgage's life.

▸ Land Registry taxes here are approx. €200

▸ Legal fees are between 1% and 2%

▸ Notary fees are between 2.5% and 3%

▸ For non-residents, registration tax is 9% (for primary residence, it is only 2%)

Rome & Milan, Italy

Beautiful areas like Rome and Milan have incredible luxury properties to offer, although the financial difficulties in Italy have turned many individuals away. Despite this, the prime real estate here still draws the attention of countless high net worth investors, as well as individuals looking to live a more peaceful life. The value for money in these areas is incredible, too, even if other locations are more prevalent in the prime property market.

The ancient city of Rome, the capital of Italy, is just one example of a location with excellent opportunities. Countless attractions draw the attention of tourists from around the globe, from the Coliseum to the Sistine Chapel and stunning artwork and architecture. The density of millionaires here may shock you, with the city being ranked 17th in the world.

While one of the financial hubs of Italy and home to the country's stock market, Milan is a city that is often known for luxury living. The prestigious restaurants and stores here blend with the culture and fantastic art, making the city unique. Asian investors funded many incredible property developments here, as Milan is quite popular among individuals of this race. The city has a worldwide appeal thanks to the culture, art, lifestyle, and (of course) prime real estate.

The Italian culture is plain to see in both Rome and Milan, although each is different in its ways, making them more popular among investors. The mortgage market's legalities here are different from most other countries. It is important to note that the government is not so welcoming to foreign investors and is not as liquid as the other locations we have mentioned. The good news is that many international lenders are offering a chance to invest in one of the region's many luxury properties.

Things to keep in mind:

▸ Sometimes, weak valuations can lead to limited financing options for overseas investors. Typically, mortgages here are only available from private banks — and they will only lend to liquid investors.

▸ Loans can be drawn on a capital repayment basis of 100% LVR. but this requires an investment of 40% of the mortgage amount to be given to the lending institution for the duration of the loan

▸ Land Registry taxes here are typically €200

- ▸ Legal fees are between 1% and 2%

- ▸ Notary fees are between 2.5% and 3%

- ▸ For non-residents, registration tax is 9% (for primary residence, it is only 2%)

Algarve and Quinta do Lago, Portugal

The community of Quinta do Lago, in the Algarve, has been famous among investors for many years now. Better yet, with the NHTR (Non-Habitual Tax Residency) scheme, Portugal is more than welcoming to foreign investors. The "Golden Visa" has encouraged more Europeans to migrate to this spectacular location. The Algarve region is well known for attracting foreign investors, especially from the UK. Thanks to the open-door policy, the demand for real estate has undoubtedly increased, with countless people wanting to invest here.

The gated community of Quinta do Lago is in the corner of the Golden Triangle — which is home to the Algarve's most prosperous locations. The region has Portugal's most expensive luxury properties. With the excellent lifestyle and natural beauty, it is easy to see why this is such a popular location for investors. One of the many things that individuals love about the Algarve is the climate — with the temperatures in summer often hitting 30°C and mild winters dropping to no less than 15°C. This allows investors to enjoy all that Algarve offers of the year.

The property market in this area has been mostly safe from Portugal's mortgage market downturn, partially because of how welcoming the Algarve is towards overseas investors. Another worth mentioning is that the region is close to a few European cities with daily flights from Faro Airport. In addition, many investors have taken the chance to enjoy the pleasures while attending to business. Many people also know the Algarve for leisure — and with several world-class golf courses and more on offer, this is the ideal place to relax.

While the property market here is doing incredibly well, there is, unfortunately, a lack of funding options available. As a result, overseas private banks offer liquidity and competition among lenders. One significant bonus of buying here is that transactions are covered by the country's strict regulations, which has resulted in an excellent and transparent mortgage market.

Things to keep in mind:

▸ Investors with the NHTR scheme will enjoy no taxes on all their income sources for the first ten years of their residency in the country.

▸ There are not any solid private banks, making property buying a little more difficult for foreign investors. Several international private banks can assist.

▸ All estate agents must be registered with the "Associacao de Mediadores Inmobiliaria" regulator. You can check an agent's credentials by contacting the "Instituto da Construcao e do Imobiliario."

▸ Legal fees and taxes here are between 6% and 10%

Lisbon, Portugal

A perfect climate, rich history, and tradition are just a few things that Lisbon offers. There are several reasons this area has been popular among property investors (both domestic and overseas), although one of them is that this city is the capital of Portugal. The pandemic had a significant impact, although the "Golden Visa" program was efficient in helping. The program, coupled with the chance to get residency, encouraged more investors to buy real estate.

The international investment in Portugal's luxury property market in Lisbon has undoubtedly seen growth over recent years. As a result, it is known for being a fantastic location in Europe for those looking for a lifestyle change. The more high-end side of the property market is not too large, but a recent study shows that demand increases. For this reason, the prices of prime real estate here are also on the rise.

One bonus is that this country has the lowest property tax rates in Europe — thanks to the proactive approach taken by the Portuguese government. The cost of living here boasts the lowest numbers in Europe, too. Many investors are attracted to the prime property market for the low-interest rates and the fact that there are no capital taxes. This is ideal for those looking to get low taxes when investing in luxury real estate. Many domestic lenders suffered from the downturn in 2008, although international mortgage lenders have stepped in. Because of this, you will find that you will often be able to negotiate for the best rates.

Residential tourism here in Portugal has seen quite a boost, with many people describing it as the "Florida of Europe". In addition, the international and domestic transport network here allows investors buying luxury properties to quickly travel to and from Lisbon to get too European (and global) business hubs. This means that Lisbon has everything an investor could need, from the incredible climate to the ability to travel to other parts of Europe when they need. So, is it any wonder that extravagant properties' demand (and prices) is steadily increasing with all this?

Things to keep in mind:

▸ Thanks to the "Golden Visa", any non-residents investing more than €500,000 on a property in Portugal can be considered for a visa (which offers five years' residency)

▸ Upon signing the sales agreement, a buyer will need to pay a deposit between 10% and 30%. This is known as the "Contrato de Promessa de Compra e Venda."

▸ You will need to notarise the agreement before you can proceed with the mortgage process, which has a cooling-off period of a week when signed.

▸ Legal fees and taxes here are between 6% and 10%

Marrakech, Morocco

Prime property investors from around the globe have long been attracted to Morocco — especially in Marrakech. In the West of Morocco, Marrakech is a central economic hub of the country, although many people love this city for its stunning views, luxurious lifestyle, and rich history. The demand for real estate here is only increasing. This includes various high-end properties, from those in the rural part of Marrakech to Medina. In addition, the ability to enjoy either city living, or a rural retreat has encouraged investors from around the globe to buy in Marrakech.

The majestic views around the city are incredible, like the Atlas Mountains in the background. Many individuals worldwide visit the international art and media festivals held here. Most find that the differences between the bustling ancient Medina region and the more rural parts of the city are staggering. Fortunately for international visitors and investors, the locals are extremely friendly towards foreigners.

There are so many reasons Marrakech is a magnet for foreign investors. There is just so much to enjoy, from the climate to the beautiful scenery. Morocco is a location that has drawn the attention of countless investors over the years because of its beauty. One of the most incredible things about Marrakech is that it offers a chance to explore the old way of life in Morocco, along with an excellent prime mortgage market. Like the many high-end golf courses, the many leisure facilities only make life here even more enjoyable.

It is often a wise idea to work with mortgage brokers who are familiar with local regulations, as buying a property is. Another thing that needs to be contemplated is that under-declaring real estate purchase prices have been causing an issue for the region. One of the significant benefits of buying here is the city's solid private banking influence, often allowing investors to ensure that they get the best rates and terms for their mortgage.

Things to keep in mind:

▸ Home loans need to be repaid in dirhams, but you do not need to open a new account in Morocco to repay your mortgage.

▸ You could use up to 12% of the purchase price to cover the costs of local taxes.

▸ Under-declaring the total price has been an issue for years now. To avoid this, it is always best to be upfront about the total amount when selling a property, despite advice or pressure from third parties.

Dubai, United Arab Emirates

Most will know of Dubai for its luxurious lifestyle and prime property market. With a significant investment from the authorities, Dubai swiftly became one of the most high-end living destinations in the world. This has led to the city having one of the most fabulous luxury property markets there is — which, alongside the incredible way of life and welcoming culture, this location is more appealing to investors. Several other parts of the UAE (United Arab Emirates) have fantastic international investment, but none are as successful as Dubai.

One of the many exciting things about this city is how the authorities have incorporated history with modern life, innovative architecture, and luxury shopping. Dubai is a location that has everything a foreign individual could want from upscale living. But unfortunately, the prices here were unsustainable, so many investors opted to leave and return to their homeland.

The prime property market in Dubai is becoming more affordable. Not only that, but more prime real estate on offer, helping to stabilise prices. Thanks to this, investors return to the property market and take advantage of high rental yields. Another bonus is that the regulatory structure of the property market here is far more modern now, too. So, where the mortgage market was once unregulated, investors and borrowers are now likely to find that loans will be far more secure.

Dubai is a magnificent destination, from the incredible skyscrapers to the manufactured Palm Islands. As a result, the city is now one of the most popular spots for foreign investors. With the high property demand, liquid mortgage market, and international investor-friendly approach the government has, there is plenty that can be taken advantage of.

Things to keep in mind:

- ▸ You will need to have personal insurance to secure a home loan — and our team here at Sherwood Finance could help you with that.

- ▸ That only UAE banks can lend in this city makes things more difficult for some, but there are several private banks with local partners.

- ▸ While individuals worldwide can invest in properties here, nationalities (like Iranians and Syrians) might have more severe LVR restrictions on their loans.

- It is crucial to understand the local procedures. Estate agents will often take care of conveyancing, but larger companies may have their own sales progression teams — which is something consider.

Barts, Caribbean

St Bartholomew is an island in the Caribbean known for being a hotspot for wealthy people. The island's population comprises many investors and celebrities — and there is a constant demand for prime real estate. For this reason alone, St Barts has one of the most popular property markets. With the island's delicious foods, fantastic beaches, beautiful sights, and so much more, it is easy to see why.

As an overseas territory of France, you will notice the French influence in this location. This has led many mortgage lenders in France to branch out to the property market in St Barts. This is ideal for those who want the most practical terms — as the more lenders there are, the more competition there is. The rivalry will continue to grow as the demand for real estate in the region increases.

It should not take long to see why St Barts is such an attractive location for investors. The beautiful climate, stunning beaches, and privacy are certainly drawn to many. In addition, investors enjoy the great tastes of the region, most of which come from fresh produce. Exclusive beach parties and incredible venues are also available for those looking for a location with active nightlife. o.

The wildlife here cannot be overlooked either, including creatures like humpback whales, sea turtles, and many more. Most will find that they can take in the breath-taking scenery while relaxing and enjoying the sunshine. There are many white-sand beaches — and these different things make prime properties in high demand. Whether you enjoy a luxurious lifestyle or a peaceful way of life closer to nature, this island is ideal for you.

Things to keep in mind:

▸ Residency is not required to invest in properties in St Barts, although most will find that the best mortgages are available to French nationals.

▸ Those who are liquid and have a range of assets may apply for an interest-only loan — although they may need to work with a private bank to do so

▸ Residents of over five years can avoid paying income tax and the wealth tax for real estate on the island.

They may not have to worry about paying VAT or other fees either.

▸ Inheritance Tax does not cover properties here.

▸ The great exchange rates offer a fantastic opportunity for overseas investors.

The Bahamas, Caribbean

There are over 700 islands in the archipelago of the Bahamas. All of which are breath taking locations. Two of the most popular are Paradise Island and Grand Bahama, both at the northern end of the region. Many of the smaller islands are mostly left alone. In the Bahamas, you can enjoy the most outstanding hotels and shopping boutiques, along with countless stunning sights (like the sea reefs, for example).

Because of the high demand for luxury real estate, it is easy to see why property prices are high. In addition, the Bahamas is often considered the ideal holiday destination for individuals — which is why this area has become such a prominent location for investors. Another reason so many people choose to invest here is that the authorities are incredibly welcoming international buyers. Because of this, they have implemented significant tax breaks, which go along nicely with the uncomplicated property market regulations. This has suited investors from around the globe, with so many people being more inclined to move here for these reasons.

Anyone who enjoys beautiful scenery will appreciate the white sandy beaches that stretch endlessly. There are several world-class golf courses here too, perfect for those who want to enjoy a little of sport during their leisure time. The national parks are known for being incredible too — and you could even have the chance to enjoy fishing or spotting dolphins by the sea. The nightlife and restaurants are fantastic, with most foods made with natural ingredients native to the Bahamas. This area is just an hour's flight away from Florida also makes it ideal for those who want to combine a life of business and relaxation.

The inviting tax environment alone is enough to entice many expats looking for a new home. The tax breaks have encouraged many investors into the area — which is why there is such a high demand for luxury properties. In addition, both international and domestic buyers benefit from the straightforward property buying process here. These advantages have not only upped the appeal but increased the competition in the lending market, although there are a few downsides that should be considered, like rental licenses. Because of this, it is always a clever idea to hire an experienced mortgage broker.

Things to keep in mind:

▸ Property investments over $250,000 have a stamp duty of 12%

▸ To rent out a property, foreign investors must apply for a license. These have annual taxes of: Less than $250.000 — 0%, $250.000 to $500,000 — 0.75%, and over $500,000 — 1%

▸ Private banking options are only available to liquid clients, with an interest reserve amount requirement equal to a year's worth of interest.

New York, United States of America

New York is one of the most prominent cities in the US. It may not be the country's capital, but most would agree that there is no other city as iconic as this one. New York is often considered the financial centre of the USA. Still, there are plenty of other things to love, like the luxury boutiques, gastronomy, and thriving culture, to name a few, all of which attract more investors. This city has so much to offer, from Manhattan to any other outer boroughs.

With the consistent demand for properties in Manhattan, it is easy to see why the prices for homes here continue to increase. Many investors are looking to buy real estate in the outer boroughs, such as the Bronx and Queens. With stunning luxury properties on offer, in recent times the mortgage market in many of these areas has improved. When investing here it is essential to know how to negotiate for the best deal and which prices are fair.

The competition has been closing between London and New York in the league table of the world's most luxurious property locations. Those who have done any research will have noticed that these two cities are terribly similar in several ways: from the real estate prices to the well-performing mortgage market for high-end properties. Unfortunately, different political situations have affected both locations. This has not stopped either of them from having a solid property market.

It is important to note that the financial market in the US differs from Europe's, with dry loans here often available for loans above $3 million. This alone draws the attention of many foreign investors to New York. But because of the pandemic, new regulations have been tightened. Despite this, the prime property market is still liquid and competitive. So, New York has plenty of potential for investors to take advantage of — both in better-known areas like Manhattan and the many luxury properties found in outer boroughs.

Things to keep in mind:

▸ In Manhattan, many of the apartment blocks are co-ops. Instead of buying an individual unit, you buy shares in the corporation, which will entitle you to a proprietary lease.

▸ Co-ops can often challenge to rent out, so look for a condominium if you want more flexibility.

▸ For $3 million+ mortgages, dry loans are readily available.

Case studies

We are proud to say that our team has helped countless clients from around the globe secure a mortgage. Whether it is a simple or more complex case, we are here to help.

Refinancing commercial property in Kings Cross

Property details

On a busy side street, the property was zoned mix use and facilitated short-term accommodation.

What did the client want?

The client was an Australian ex-pat, living and working in the UK. They were looking to offer their property security to raise funds for future investments.

Key points

Years ago, many mainstream lenders changed their view on accepting foreign income for servicing calculation.

What did we do?

We worked the scenario with multiple lenders and provided a suitable solution.

Difficulties along the way

The valuation came in lower than expected.

The end results

Although the client received less cash out because of the valuation, we achieved a satisfactory result.

Refinance of a hotel in London

Property details

They assigned us with assisting an individual in refinancing their hotel development in London.

What did the client want?

They were hoping to find a better loan term than their current bank gave them.

Difficulties along the way

The hotel was a fresh development and had not been open to guests for long. Because of this, many banks were sceptical of the client's ability to repay their loan. To make matters worse, the fluctuation of the economic landscape in the UK had harmed the client's credit.

What did we do?

We searched around for the ideal lender – one that our client had not yet encountered. The lender had the best rates available and a chance to have a strong business relationship, suitable for getting excellent terms for the client's future investments.

The result

We negotiated for a capital raise a 60% LTV, allowing the client more freedom for their plans on developments for the property. We secured a rate of 5% over five years for a 10-year term.

Refinance of a luxury property in Amsterdam

Property details

A home along a canal in Amsterdam.

What did the client want?

The client was an Australian resident who wanted a hundred per cent finance with minimal assets required.

What did we do?

We negotiated with a lender, and they agreed to hold the client's money in EUR and USD, which would help to increase the value of their AUM and the security.

The result

After this, we secured an LVR of 100%, with a rate of 1.6% pa over the next five years.

Property finance for a high-end apartment in Dublin

Property details

Four-bedroom apartment

What did the client want?

The client was an American resident looking for the lowest rates on an interest-only loan. They wanted to work with a private bank to take custody of their stock for the AUM requirements instead of cash.

What did we do?

With access to a vast network of lenders, we soon found one willing to work with our client. They were also prepared to take custody of the securities if necessary – and we did all this while still getting a fixed rate of 1.75% for the duration of the mortgage.

The result

Our client ended up with a 95.5% LVR with a meagre fixed-rate interest-only loan and an AUM of €2,900,00.

Equity release for business expansion

Business details

The business was an educational facility in Surrey.

What did the client want?

The client was a UK resident who had previously worked with our team at Sherwood Finance. They had wanted to sell their company for £6m a year ago – although they instead opted to continue with the business to expand on it a little more.

Difficulties along the way

Since it was a loan backed by the client's business and not an asset lends, there was not any reliable security we offered. Most lenders are a little apprehensive about agreeing to provide a loan under these circumstances.

What did we do?

We work with countless different lenders, so it did not take us long to find one that would help us. This one specialised in funding businesses that are trying to grow – and after negotiating and discussing specific details about the client and their needs, we agreed everyone was happy with it.

The result

The lender was keen to work with growing businesses to get our client a loan of £2.5m unsecured. This allowed them to buy out a 10% shareholder and keep complete control of their company – and with the remaining £1.4 million, they could grow their business.

Re mortgage on a self-built property

Property details

The property was self-built and had six bedrooms. It was a detached and unique property, but it repelled most lenders a timber frame and SIP panels.

What did the client want?

The client was self-employed and wanted to Re-mortgage and repay their brother who had loaned them money to finish the property, and they wanted as much as they could borrow.

Difficulties along the way

Although lenders only used her salary, our client's wife was a 32% shareholder. They used the client's new profits and their latest year's salary, which allowed us to maximise the loan amount. A flexible approach was the key to our success.

What did we do?

We needed to prove that our client's expenses were at a minimum, so even though they needed more than the ordinary 5x income. they could afford it. And fortunately, we could contact a lender who understood and was happy to work with our client.

The result

We maximised the loan amount, resulting in an interest-only deal with 6x income.

Property refinancing in the South of France

Key points:

▸ Refinancing required: €2 million

▸ Reason to refinance: A home improvement project

Property details

The £5.4m property was valued at precisely that and would be the loan's central security.

What did the client want?

The client was an American resident living in France, and they were looking to refinance their home for a renovation/business project.

Difficulties along the way

There were a few complications with this situation: European leaders do not be very negotiable with American borrowers. With this in mind, we opted to look to private banks instead – as most private banks are more flexible for different nationalities and reasons for refinancing.

What did we do?

This was not as simple as a standard mortgage, so we had to negotiate with various contacts in the private banking sector to find the ideal refinancing loan for our client.

The result

We secured a €4 mild interest-only mortgage with an LVR of 75%. It was a fixed-rate loan of 1.5%, plus Euribor.

Bridging Loan in Sydney

Property details

Within Sydney's central business district and nearby the cobbled streets of the rocks, the real estate was on a historic road, with proximity to major infrastructure and entertainment venues.

What did the client want?

The refusal stranded the purchaser just days before the settlement date. He was heading towards legal and financial trouble.

Difficulties along the way

After submitting the application, the lodgement of a hefty court judgement alerted the lender on the borrower's credit file

Key points

Several specialists are bridging lenders out there. Many can offer funding outside the traditional mortgage, only available through the best finance brokers.

What did we do?

We introduced a specialist lender that prides itself on being efficient in quick settlements.

The end results

We settled the transaction one day after the scheduled date. Because we facilitated bridging finance, they incurred increased costs. But the clients understood, and we refinanced them into standard mortgage terms after the court judgment.

Who we are?

Here at Sherwood Finance, our group of mortgage brokers offers a wide variety of services. We aim to help individuals with mortgage funding. This encompasses several monetary contracts.

We have access to over a hundred investors because of our independent status, including several lenders, from traditional banks to private loan companies. We can categorise our services.

▶ Bridging and emergency finance

▶ Commercial and development finance

▶ Property purchases

▶ Property refinancing

▶ Releasing equity from a property

Our team of specialist financiers are here to offer advice and arrange mortgages for investors, regardless of their financial landscape. Our quality, priced services can help anyone, whether they need traditional or more unique mortgage funding. We have worked with a broad range of individuals over the years, and we are sure that we will be able to help regardless of your financial situation, or even your background.

To get the ideal plan of action for your property financing needs, our specialists can help you. If you are looking to hire a team of experienced advisers, we are confident that you will want to consider our qualified experts. Because of our independent status, we are not obligated to work with any lending companies. Which is why we negotiate with countless different recognised lenders worldwide. This allows us to search various potential deals and terms to find the best one. As a result, we have been able to help countless individuals, from those with a simple financial background to those who need a more bespoke home loan. Sherwood Finance is often more than equipped to help with your unique situation, as we work with individuals across the globe.

We take the time to understand our clients, what they need and want, and their current situation to get an idea of the best plan of action. Then, with the information we need, we can work on sourcing market rates and helping them further into the process.

If you want to find out about mortgage rates and loan to value ratios or better understand your options, you will find what you are looking for here. Will give you an idea of the most worthwhile bespoke arrangements (important to note that these will vary depending on the circumstances). Each enquiry is unique to us, which is why we strive to offer rewarding terms for every case.

Contact: daniel@sherwoodfinance.co.uk

Glossary of terms

Arrangement fees

When lenders charge for the effort of providing financing to a borrower, this fee can vary from one lender to another.

Auction

An auctioneer conducts a sales process in public.

Auctioneer

A profession that oversees the sale of real estate or other items whereby persons become purchasers by competition in public view, the sale favours the highest bidder.

Balance

A statement begins with your last statement's balance, which is the amount you had within your account at the end of the previous report.

Bankruptcy

A legal concept that you would be best to avoid. Also known as Insolvency, this occurs when an individual cannot meet their financial obligations within a reasonable period or if their liabilities exceed their assets.

Bid

A method of purchasing real estate at auction is by an offering.

Caveat

A property caveat is a claim to a property as a legal document. Creating a caveat allows both parties to claim their share of interest. Until the caveat is settled, no further transactions can be registered against the title.

Capital Gains Tax

If you sell an asset such as investment property for a profit, in some locations you are subject to capital gains tax (CGT). At the end of the fiscal year, they add the capital gain to your income tax.

Cheque

Cheques detail any amount of money that is withdrawn since account holders often write the cheque to pay someone. This includes the number on the cheque and the amount taken out.

Court judgement

If a person cannot repay their creditors, creditors can get a judgment in court.

Commercial tenants

Commercial, industrial, and retail properties are standard in arranging long-term leases. In addition, outgoings are negotiated but passed onto the tenant.

Commitment fee

They add a fee onto a loan to compensate a lender for their commitment to offering to fund.

Company secretary

A secretary's responsibility is to circulate agendas and other documents to directors, shareholders, and auditors and make correct minutes of shareholder and director's meetings and resolutions.

Contract of sale

An agreement includes the terms, conditions signed, dated, and witnessed by all related parties.

Conveyance

When real estate is transferred from one party to another, in real estate, this could be when a seller transfers the ownership of a property to a buyer.

Collateral

Collateral is protection to mitigate the risks involved with lending.

Credit

While this refers to several aspects of lending, most used to describe a contract agreement where an individual receives money and repays the lender by a predetermined date (usually with an additional interest fee).

Credit score

Used by lenders to decide whether to accept funding applications based on the risk associated with the borrower. Also referred to as a credit rating.

Development Approval

Local town planning authorities offer written approval for a project, prepared by the developer's or landowner's consultants, allowing the project to move forward as per the development plan.

Deposit

The amount of money needed to be paid upfront as part of the loan agreement. The amount specified can often vary depending on a variety of circumstances.

Division of Property

fair distribution, or property division, divides property rights and obligations between divorced or De facto spouses and business partners.

Director

An individual that manages a company's operations, with the ability to exercise the business' powers for whatever needs it may have.

Economy

A summary of goods, services produced, distributed, and sold within a region or country.

Equity

Property equity is the difference between the remaining debt and the asset's capital value in question.

Exchange of Contracts

When a seller and buyer sign a copy of the sale contract and then exchange these documents, create a binding agreement for the sale of real estate on agreed terms. They then bound the parties to proceed to settlement, subject to any cooling-off period that may apply.

First mortgage

When a borrower uses the property as security for the first time as collateral for a loan, as usual, if they do not meet the mortgage repayments as agreed, the lender can seize the security.

Financial position

An organisation's financial position refers to its assets, liabilities, and equity balances. In a broader sense, the concept can describe the financial condition, which is determined by analysing and comparing its financial statements.

Guarantor

In property development transactions, lenders could require additional security to reduce their risk should the developer default on a loan. This guarantee can take various forms, from cash to property.

Gross Realised Value

In property construction, the Gross Realisation Value is the gross sales (or GST (Good and Services Tax) exclusive value of the property) upon the completion of the project. Also known as GRV.

Initial Public Offering

When a company raises capital from public investors by offering shares of a corporation in a public share issuance, we often abbreviate it to IPO (Initial Public Offering).

Interest rate

The amount of interest charged on a loan, in proportion to the amount borrowed, allows a bank or lender to profit when distributing funds.

Investment property

A real estate buy intends to earn rental income or capital gain.

Indicative offer

Lenders often show or suggest that the offer may proceed if they meet conditions, also known as a conditional offer.

Joint and severally

Where all parties are equally accountable for the full terms of the agreement, they have entered. For example, in a personal liability case, each party will pursue to repay the entire amount owed.

Lawyer

A lawyer is someone who practices law and deals with legal issues. A lawyer provides legal advice and represents people in court.

Land Banking

Usually refers to financing secured for the acquisition and holding of developmental sites with no certainty of rapid development.

Legal fees

Upon completing the buy, the solicitor or conveyancer will charge a fee for the legal work carried out during buying. Most solicitors charge a flat fee regardless of the property's value.

Letter of Offer

When a lender issues a finance offer to a borrower, it can be accepted or rejected depending on the borrower in question acceptance.

Lease agreements

They make lease agreements between the property owner and tenant to occupy real estate.

Loan to Value

All lenders use a Loan to Value Ratio to assess risk when they consider funding and can have a tremendous impact on the terms offered, abbreviated to LTV (loan to values) or LVR (Loan to Value Ratio).

Litigation

When disputes are resolved in court through litigation, unless the parties settle before trial, a judge may make the final decision for the parties in litigation.

Liabilities

Liabilities are obligations between two parties that have not yet been completed or repaid.

Mortgage

A debt passed onto a borrower from a lender secured by a property.

Mortgagee sale

In the event of a default by the mortgagor, the mortgagee claims the security and resells to avoid economic losses.

Mortgagor

A borrower (individual or company) has an interest in a property through a mortgage as security for credit advancement.

Net Realised Value

They reduced the asset value realised on the sale because of standard deductions. Therefore, it is often abbreviated to NRV.

Non-conforming loans

The term non-conforming loan refers to lending that does not meet the criteria for bank financing. There are a variety of reasons for this.

Non-recourse loan

When a lender can seize the security if a borrower defaults on their payments, the difference from standard scenarios is that the lender cannot get further compensation, even if the collateral covers the total unpaid loan.

Offshore

Ideal for overseas investors, most offshore financing options are available for competitive prices and offer enticing sums of money. The general, the applications to be considered are company borrowers.

Passed in

If the owner's reserve price has not been met and they do not sell a property at auction; therefore, passed in.

Periodic lease

Typical with residential, a tenant continues to rent and occupy the property beyond the expiration of the lease agreement.

Presales

A lender will want a certain number of presales to reduce their risks. While the percentage of pre-sold units is not set, funding can vary slightly from one lender to another.

Principal and Interest Mortgage

A standard mortgage, with the difference that monthly repayments are part capital and part interest.

Property Acquisition

When legal ownership or rights over real estate are transferred, the rules may vary from one state to another.

Property Maintenance

Property owners will need to decide about building works and maintenance. The agent managing your property will manage and looking after the property. This includes marketing your property, collecting rent and fixing any issues.

Progress Payments

As the construction progresses, lenders drawdown payments in stages. Therefore, the lender needs to report the work completed by its Quantity Surveyor to compare the completed work as part of the loan agreement.

Property Settlement

A legal process facilitated by the legal and financial representatives of the purchaser and the seller. Settlement occurs when ownership is passed from the seller to the buyer. Typically, the settlement date is determined in the contract of sale by the vendor.

Profit

When the financial earnings of a business activity exceed the amount needed for the costs, taxes, etc., this could be when a company buys something and sells it for a higher price.

Preferred equity

Investments or loans exceeding the level associated with project and deemed debt but not taking part in equal ranking equity.

Rescind

To discontinue a contract of sale.

Reserve Price

The vendor agrees upon the minimum acceptable price before the Auction.

Residential tenants

In most cases, residential leases last for one year; any shorter would be costly for the property owner for re-tenanting costs such as marketing, rental income delays and re-letting fees to the agent.

Recourse

If the debt obligation is not honoured, a lender may get a borrower's security. A full recourse is when a lender can take additional assets to repay the entire unpaid debt.

Receipt

A note of any money that is deposited into your account. It also known as paid-in or credits.

Settlement Date

The last part of the process is whereby the purchaser completes the payment of the contract price to the seller, and they transferred legal possession to the purchaser.

Share certificates

A share certificate is a document that is issued by a company that sells shares. An investor receives a share certificate upon purchasing a certain number of shares and as a record of ownership.

Joint tenants

Joint tenancy is the default type of shared ownership. There is no property division between the joint owners; each owns one hundred per cent of the property. Legal ownership of the property passes to the surviving joint owner when a joint owner dies.

Statement of Position

According to their assets and liabilities, companies or individual positions show the current net equity position.

Security

Security on a mortgage is essential because it reduces the risk a lender takes on when providing a loan. Suppose a loan is backed by property, for example. Then, if the borrower defaults on repayments, the lender may seize the property to claim the outstanding debt.

Share certificates

Whenever a company sells shares on the market, it issues shares certificates. As proof of ownership and as a record of the purchase, they issue shares certificates to shareholders.

Shareholders

A person or business that owns a share in a company's stock. They can receive capital gains, take capital losses, and they may receive dividend payments. They are equity owners and have the same benefits and drawbacks as Directors.

Second mortgage

A borrower can offer their real estate as collateral a second time to another lender while the first still has finance secured. As a result, the subsequent lender takes a second charge over the property.

Senior Debt

The registered mortgage holds the property's first ranking for a primary mortgage or principal debt. Developers often prefer senior debt as the margins are lower since banks or significant mortgage funds typically offer senior debt.

Tax returns

Tax authorities use this process to assess a taxpayer's liability based on their annual income personal circumstances and include corporate entities.

Tenants in common

A joint ownership arrangement exists when multiple individuals own the same property, but neither has the right of one hundred per cent ownership of the property. For example, if you do not make a will, you can "will" your share of the property to a beneficiary of your choice.

Valuer

A company appointed to conduct the assessment of the current market value of the real estate.

Variation

To change or alter the conditions of the contract of sale.

Valuation

Not to be confused with make sure an appraisal, as a valuation provides a more correct and recognised property value.

Vendor

In a real estate transaction, a person(s) or entity sells the property.

Quantity Surveyor

A qualified individual that examines costs associated with the building costs. Market conditions impact labour costs and material suppliers with the DA (development approval). Lenders also keep them to make sure that the project is correctly costed.

Yield

A sign of income by percentage earned on real estate. It is Calculated by the received net income and the market value of the real estate.

Zoning

The local council planning controls current and future development, including residential, business, and industrial uses.

**For further information
about Sherwood Finance:**

Call us 1800 743 796

head to the website
www.sherwoodfinance.com.au

follow us on Facebook, Instagram
and Twitter.

Lightning Source UK Ltd.
Milton Keynes UK
UKHW050608080223
416654UK00001B/35